Original title:
Ballads of Brambleberry Bog

Copyright © 2025 Creative Arts Management OÜ
All rights reserved.

Author: Ronan Whitfield
ISBN HARDBACK: 978-1-80567-382-8
ISBN PAPERBACK: 978-1-80567-681-2

Fables in the Flickering Light

In the heart of the bog, where the critters convene,
A frog donned a crown, for a royal routine.
He sang to the moon with a voice so absurd,
Got tangled in reeds, oh, how the frogs stirred!

With a twirl and a splash, he fell in a pond,
A fish popped his head up and gave a response.
"Your reign is a laugh, dear amphibian king,
Might I suggest you stick to the spring?"

Then a hedgehog arrived, with a hat made of twine,
Declared he was prince of the bramble for fun.
He juggled acorns while dancing around,
But tripped on a root and fell with a sound!

As laughter erupted from all of the crowd,
They cheered for the antics, joyfully loud.
In this bog full of giggles, a lesson was found,
That joy is the crown, forever renowned!

Fluttering Petals under the Veil

In a garden where petals just love to play,
The bees wear sunglasses, buzzing away.
The daisies gossip on how to sway,
While butterflies twirl, oh what a display!

A breeze blows a riddle, quite cleverly thrown,
Tickling the roses, a secret well-known.
They whisper in colors, in whispers they've grown,
Each petal a giggle, each stem a sweet moan.

The Fawn's Fragile Courage

A fawn wanted to leap, but felt quite meek,
It jumped at the sound of a twig's little creak.
With its heart all aflutter, it tried not to squeak,
Running in circles for a week on the peak.

The wise old owl hooted, "Just show them your style!"
With a skip and a hop, it went half a mile.
All critters around gathered, grinning with guile,
The shy little fawn, now the star of the aisle.

Harmonies of the Hidden Hollow

In a hollow where shadows dance and prance,
    The critters hold a midnight chance.
With owls that wail and raccoons that prance,
    They form a band for a whimsical dance.

The squirrels strum strings, the rabbits hum,
While frogs play the drums, oh what a thrum!
    The fireflies twinkle, providing the glum,
    Together they laugh, ignoring the scum.

The Riddle of the Reluctant River

In a river that dodges and weaves so sly,
A fish told a joke that made frogs leap high.
The rafts refuse to float on by,
For they laugh so hard, they almost cry.

The turtles spin tales of splashes and fun,
While crabs clack their claws in the sun.
But the river just giggles, always on the run,
Pranking the banks till the day is done.

Shadows of the Weeping Fern

In the shade where ferns do hide,
A frog in a hat takes a slippery slide.
He leaps with a ribbit, a humorous flair,
While squirrels roll chuckling, in the cool, crisp air.

A rabbit named Chuck wears shoes far too tight,
He hops and he stumbles, it's quite a sight.
With each clumsy bounce, he squeaks in delight,
While fireflies giggle, they light up the night.

The Song of the Hidden Grove

In the grove where shadows dance,
A raccoon steals cookies — bold little prance.
He nibbles and giggles, all cheeks full of crumbs,
While owls just hoot, 'Look at those chums!'

A hedgehog in boots sings a tune out of key,
His voice makes the bushes all tremble with glee.
The trees shake their leaves, they can't help but sway,
As the moon cracks a smile, brightening the play.

Adventures in the Wistful Wilderness

Down in the meadow, where the daisies twirl,
A turtle's slow dance makes the critters whirl.
With a wink and a spin, oh what a sight,
The bees buzz along, adding musical light.

A goat with a top hat juggles juicy pears,
As lizards applaud from their sun-soaked chairs.
The breeze carries laughter, as they start to cheer,
For every silly moment, they hold so dear.

Legends of the Gossamer Glade

In the glade where mischief blooms,
A fairy tells tales of the wiliest grooms.
With glimmers of gold and a playful snap,
She tickles the toes of the gnomes in a nap.

A fox in pajamas holds a cheese soirée,
Where raccoons trade secrets and nibble away.
The laughter it echoes, through twilight so bright,
As the stars giggle on in sheer pure delight.

Lament of the Wandering Willows

Willows weep with laughter's grace,
Their branches tickle, a playful race.
They sway and bend in silly cheer,
Whispering jokes only trees can hear.

The breeze joins in with a gentle sigh,
As leaves hang low, they dare to fly.
Caught in vines, they twist and spin,
Lamenting joy, where trouble's thin.

Nearby, frogs sport a grand parade,
In crowns of lily, their antics displayed.
With leaps and croaks, they bring delight,
A swampy circus, oh what a sight!

Nature giggles at life's little quirks,
Around the bog, every critter works.
Together they dance, a woodland band,
In the land where laughter takes a stand.

Secrets of the Swirling Tide

The brook babbles tales, mischievous and bright,
With fish that wink under flickering light.
They plot a prank on an unsuspecting frog,
Who dreams of croaking a great cosmic blog.

The water spins secrets, round and round,
While turtles gossip without a sound.
A splash here, a ripple there,
It's just the current's playful flair.

A raccoon dips in, curious to see,
If the tales are as funny as they claim to be.
With a splash and a dash, oh what a sight,
They all tumble in, laughter taking flight!

In the swirling waters, joy makes its bed,
With creatures chiming tunes in mirth instead.
The secrets revealed, so funny and free,
In jests of the tide, pure jubilee.

A Forgotten Melody of the Night

Under a moon that winks and plays,
Crickets chirp in whimsical ways.
They sing forgotten tunes so bright,
While fireflies twirl, a comical sight.

Owl hoots softly, a wise old sage,
With notes like whispers, they turn the page.
He chuckles low at the jests of night,
As stars twinkle back in sheer delight.

The shadows dance with a romping glee,
Each rustle and stir, a joyous decree.
Bats play tag in the cool night air,
While lanterns on trees fumble, unaware.

In this dark symphony of vibrant flair,
Every giggle hangs thick like the air.
A melody forgotten, yet so divine,
Turns the night into one grand punchline.

Time's Tapestry in the Thicket

In the thicket's heart where minutes collide,
The hedgehogs roll and squirrels abide.
Time unravels with a tickle and tease,
As seasons change with the greatest of ease.

The bumblebees buzz in a frantic chase,
Searching for nectar, a sweetened embrace.
With pollen on noses, they fumble and fall,
Leaving flowers laughing, a bright floral ball.

Old trees gossip in the soothing breeze,
Sharing secrets like whispered leaves.
With each rustle, they jest and poke,
A tapestry woven with nature's joke.

In the thicket's maze, where time tickles slow,
Funny moments sprout wherever you go.
Here, joy stitches memories with ease,
In nature's laughter, the heart finds peace.

The Glistening Traces of Dusk's Embrace

In the gloaming, critters prance,
Chasing shadows, lost in chance.
Fireflies dance with jester's glee,
While frogs croak jokes beneath the tree.

A squirrel's leap, so bold and spry,
Tripped on roots, oh my, oh my!
The moon winks down on this grand show,
As whispers tickle where the reeds grow.

The owls hoot tales of yesteryear,
Of slippery snails that brought them cheer.
While crickets sing a serenade,
To tease the shadows that parade.

In dusk's embrace, laughter softens,
Mistakes became grand, as fun often often.
The night's a stage, no need to fret,
For every blunder, there's joy to get.

Chronicles of the Creaking Canopy

Beneath the boughs, the limbs do sway,
As wise old trees share tales each day.
With creaks and groans, they muse and sigh,
Of windy pranks that made them try.

A raccoon once tried to climb so high,
But slipped and tumbled with a cry.
The branches laughed, they swung and bent,
At his mischief, their hearts were content.

The squirrels have secrets, up they go,
Crafty little thieves, stealing the show.
Yet one got caught in a swingy mess,
His face, a picture of sheer distress.

The tales are spun from leafy lore,
Where every mishap opens a door.
With giggles shared in the sunlit glade,
Nature's jesters serenade.

The Enchanted Secrets of the Overgrown

Tangles weave in the wild, wild wood,
A messy scene, as it certainly should.
Where fairies trip on their long, green gowns,
And giggles echo in sparkly crowns.

A wayward vine wrapped round a bug,
He spun like crazy, oh what a shrug!
With pixies laughing from their flight,
At how he danced in the pale moonlight.

The ferns hide tales of those who roam,
Adventurous insects, they call it home.
And when a hedgehog takes a stroll,
He bumps and rolls, oh, what a goal!

Secrets hidden in leafy beds,
Where nature's laughter is gently spread.
So if you wander, take a glance,
You might just see a plant's own dance!

Tales of the Twilight Tides

At twilight's edge, the water's grin,
Reflects the mischief, where tales begin.
The waves, they splash, and giggle bright,
As crabs put on a comical fight.

A fish decided it would brave,
To leap through foam, so proud and brave.
But flopped right down, with such a splat,
While seaweed chuckled, "What was that?"

The gulls above share jokes for free,
About the antics of fish and sea.
They swoop and dive, with laughter loud,
Underneath the silver shroud.

When darkness falls, the fun won't cease,
For tide pools hold a wacky lease.
With crabs that dance and shells that sing,
The nighttime antics, oh what a fling!

Mysteries of the Forgotten Fen

In the swamps where frogs sing loud,
A turtle wears a purple shroud.
It claims to know the secrets deep,
Of stolen socks and dreams that creep.

A cricket dances on a log,
Beside a snoozing sleepy dog.
He dreams of being a great stand-up,
But wakes to find he's lost his cup.

A warty newt tells tales so tall,
Of treasure chests beyond the thrall.
But when the seekers come to look,
They only find a soggy book.

The fog rolls in, the night is spry,
With whispers of a dancing pie.
But when you chase that crusty treat,
It rolls away with nimble feet.

A Puddle's Dream

There once was a puddle, round and wide,
Who wished to be more than a place to slide.
It dreamed of being a grand waterpark,
With splashing kids and a giant shark.

But every time the sun blazed bright,
The puddle shrank out of sheer fright.
It splashed some mud but the kids just laughed,
'This isn't a shark!' was their harsh draft.

One rainy day, the sky was gray,
The kids returned for a splashy play.
'Look at this puddle, it's our best friend,'
And so the puddle's dreams did blend.

With raindrops tapping, the fun did bloom,
Turning that puddle into a room.
Where laughter echoed and joy endured,
The puddle smiled, its heart assured.

Rustling Leaves and Faded Starlight

In the forest where whispers dwell,
A squirrel thought he could cast a spell.
With acorns piled on his tiny head,
He sought to wake the moon instead.

But all he got was a sleepy sigh,
As stars blinked down from the midnight sky.
'No magic here, just fuzzy dreams,'
The wind replied with giggly schemes.

A raccoon joined with a pie in claw,
'Who's up for mischief? Give me a law!'
They plotted pranks for the next full night,
Chasing shadows, causing delight.

The leaves laughed loud, the branches danced,
As critters pranced, and stars were pranced.
They tiptoed through with giggles in tow,
In a silent disco, put on a show.

The Fable of the Wayward Wanderer

There was a wanderer, lost in glee,
Who followed his nose to a drippy tree.
It promised him pies and a chocolate lake,
But led him straight to a pranky snake.

With every step, confusion grew,
Through tangled roots and a dance of dew.
He called for help, but who could hear?
Just giggling bees and a raucous deer.

At last, he found a path to go,
Where mushrooms glowed in a feathery row.
He dined on twigs and sipped from air,
Claiming the forest was simply fair.

So if you wander, take heed, my friend,
Adventure's waiting 'round each bend.
But beware of sneaky critters so sly,
Who'll turn your dreams to a buddy's pie!

The Dusk's Embrace of Evergreens

When dusk arrives, the trees all sway,
The critters dance, come out to play.
With acorns tossed and shadows long,
They sing a tune, oh so wrong!

A squirrel with a hat, so bright,
Climbs up the oak, what a sight!
While raccoons juggle berries round,
They laugh and tumble on the ground.

The owls hoot jokes, a comic spree,
While hedgehogs giggle, oh so free.
Amidst the ferns, a party brews,
With every critter sharing news!

So when the sun dips low and fades,
Join in the fun, the forest parades.
In evergreens, with laughter's grace,
The night unfolds, a joyous place!

Nightingales in the Gloom

Nightingales sing out in the dark,
Their tunes get lost, a funny lark.
They try to charm the drifting mist,
But crickets chime in, none can resist!

A cat with dreams of catching flies,
Sits in the gloom with wide-eyed sighs.
But every pounce goes awry,
As fireflies tease, just flutter by.

The stars above start to giggle too,
As shadows waltz, with a curtsy, woo!
A hedgehog rolls, a comical spin,
With every twist, the laughs begin.

So if you wander, hear the sweet strain,
Of nightingale antics, it's quite insane!
In the gloom, where the humor flows,
The night embraces, and laughter grows!

The Thistle's Tear

There lived a thistle with prickly pride,
She wore her thorns, a fierce guide.
But when a bee buzzed right on by,
She tried to hide; oh my, oh my!

With tears of dew, she called out loud,
"Why, oh why, can't I join the crowd?"
But daisies laughed, in colors bright,
While thistle fretted, tucked in tight.

The breeze took pity, and gave a nudge,
"Come play with us! Just give a hug!"
But thistle sighed, and cringed away,
"I'm prickly, friends, what more can I say?"

Yet one fine day, through giggles and cheer,
She let them close, it was worth the fear.
With all the blooms, she found her glee,
A prickle here, a friend, oh me!

The Crow's Lamentation

A crow perched high with a puffed-up pride,
Cawed out loudly, with wings spread wide.
"Why don't the woods respect my style?
I'm dark and dapper, with a smile!"

But rabbits snickered, tails in a twist,
"Your caw is loud, but you just missed!
A cat will steal the show tonight,
You'll end up in the trees, in a fright!"

The crow rolled eyes, a dramatic flair,
"I'm noble! Watch me, if you dare!"
But as he dove for a tasty crumb,
He tripped on a stick and went feet-up! Thud!

With caws of laughter echoing round,
He joined the jesters on the ground.
So if you hear a crow complain,
Just know he's part of the laughing chain!

Murmurs of the Listening Fog

In the thick of the fog, a voice once spoke,
It asked for a hat—what a funny joke!
With whiskers and winks, the mist danced around,
As laughter erupted from far and abound.

A frog in a tux made quite the display,
He croaked a weird tune that chased woes away.
The trees giggled softly, the owls rolled their eyes,
While shadows did shimmy in hazy surprise.

The whispers grew louder, a chorus of cheer,
Tiny bugs formed a band, drawing near.
With banjo and kazoo, they played through the night,
While everyone chuckled at the froggy delight.

So if you should wander where the fog likes to play,
Expect silly antics to brighten your day.
For in bramble and mist, where the echoes collide,
All mischief resides, just in laughter's sweet tide.

The Labyrinth of Lingering Echoes

In a maze of old echoes, a squirrel did run,
He chased after giggles—oh, what silly fun!
With each twist and turn, the laughter grew loud,
As thickets of chuckles formed quite the crowd.

A hedgehog with glasses kept reading aloud,
Maps to the paths where the pranks were avowed.
He tripped on a twig, and oh, how he spun,
The echoes all chuckled at his clumsy run.

In corners of twilight, choices grew thick,
With whispers of whoopees and laughter's own trick.
Each turn held surprises, each squeal was a spark,
As shadows played tag in the deepening dark.

And if ever you wander where echoes carry on,
Just follow the chuckles until they are gone.
For within that quaint maze, oh, the joy it bestows,
Is a tickle of laughter wherever one goes.

The Fen's Embrace

In a fen full of giggles, a duck took a dive,
Waddling with style, he felt oh-so alive.
A reach for a lily, oh splish and a splash,
The flowers erupted, their petals did clash.

With frogs croaking jokes that left everyone bold,
Charming their friends with each story retold.
The cattails were shaking, they joined in the jest,
As smiles bloomed brightly, it felt like a fest.

A shy ol' snail brought a snail shell of dreams,
Inside it contained all the funniest schemes.
He whispered to crickets, they chimed in with ease,
Creating a sonnet that danced on the breeze.

So step into the fen where the good times convene,
And let laughter's embrace be the sweetest routine.
For in muck and in mire, life's humor does cling,
In a cauldron of chuckles, it's joy that we bring.

Gossamer Threads of the Evergreen

In the branches of conifers, threads spun so bright,
With whispers of humor that danced in the light.
A rabbit in sneakers was racing the breeze,
Chasing after the giggles that rustled the trees.

There's a parrot who rapped, a twist in his beak,
With punchlines that fluttered, quite bold and unique.
The pines they were chuckling, swaying to tune,
While raccoons held court under the watchful moon.

A fox in a scarf told tall tales by the brook,
While fireflies twinkled, each one a light book.
With stories of mishaps, oh how they did flow,
Through gossamer threads, the mirth became glow.

So wander among evergreens, find laughter's key,
For in giggling whispers, life's jokes roam so free.
In threads of delight, let your worries unwind,
As you bask in the joy that the forest can find.

Whirlpools of Echoed Dreams

In a pond where the frogs all croon,
A turtle danced to a silly tune.
The fish wore hats that were way too tall,
And the brave little snail said, 'Let's stall!'

They twirled and spun with no care in sight,
Chasing shadows that giggled in flight.
Bubbles of laughter burst in the air,
While frogs debated who'd win the fair.

With every splash and every cheer,
The dragonflies buzzed and said, 'Oh dear!'
But the party raged on, wild and grand,
In the whirling waters, they made their stand.

So join the fun by the edge of the stream,
Where nothing is real, but all is a dream.
The echoes of laughter ring loud and bright,
In the whirlpools of pure, crazy delight.

The Firefly's Farewell

A firefly flicked with a zany cheer,
He said, 'Watch my dance, I'm the star here!'
He twirled and spun with a glimmering glow,
But tripped on a beetle—oh no, oh no!

With a dizzy little laugh, he took to the sky,
Flashing bright signals to the clouds nearby.
His pals in the dark couldn't help but snicker,
As he wobbled about, a dazzling flicker.

Then up came the moon, with a grin so wide,
Said, 'Don't worry, little, I've got your guide!'
Together they danced on that starry stage,
While the marsh critters squealed at his blazing rage.

As dawn began creeping with a sleepy yawn,
The firefly bowed, then silently shone.
He left quite the tale on that whimsical night,
A spark in the dark, a comical sight.

The Sylvan Symphony

In a glen where the trees loved to sway,
The critters gathered for the fun play.
A squirrel with a flute, a crow with a drum,
And a hedgehog who danced to the beat of a hum.

With a tap of the feet and a wink of an eye,
The music inspired the clouds to fly.
The rabbits stomped, the possums swayed,
While the wise old owl stayed unafraid.

The deer pranced in time, a sight so neat,
All the woodland creatures moved to the beat.
Even the fish in the stream joined the show,
With bubbles and splashes putting on a glow.

But soon came the rain, with a pitter-pat sound,
Everyone squeaked, 'We're soaking the ground!'
They laughed as they twirled in a wet jubilee,
Creating a symphony, wild and free.

Murmurs of the Misty Hollow

In a hollow where whispers curl and play,
The wind told secrets in a teasing way.
A raccoon peeked out, ears pricked with glee,
Laughing at shadows, a riddle to see.

The mist wore a wink, fluffed up at the seams,
As the crickets chirped out their mischievous themes.
A snail told a tale that was very absurd,
Of a cat who thought it could fly like a bird.

The owls roared in laughter, deep in the trees,
While the frogs ribbited jokes on the breeze.
The fireflies linked arms, forming a line,
And twirled round the mushrooms, saying, 'Oh, divine!'

So in the mist, where silliness thrives,
The pulse of the hollow thrums and jives.
With whispers and giggles, they dance 'til it's light,
Murmurs of joy in the magical night.

The Fox's Secret Trail

Down by the swamp, where the tall grass sways,
A fox spins tales of whimsical ways.
With a wiggle of tail, he dances with glee,
Avoiding the puddles, how clever is he!

His secret trail, where the mushrooms grow,
He tiptoes around like a clever old pro.
Giggling frogs join in, they peek from the reeds,
Together they plot all their mischief and deeds.

But one day a bear took a stroll down the line,
He stumbled on fox, oh what a decline!
A chase full of laughter, they tumbled and rolled,
Font of mishaps, their stories retold!

In the twilight hour, they share with delight,
How they outwitted shadows dancing at night.
With chuckles and snickers, they finally part,
The fox and the bear, both a little bit smart!

Lights of the Dusky Vale

In the vale where the owls like to hoot and to glide,
The light shapes a story that they never hide.
With candles of fireflies flickering bright,
The critters all gather to frolic at night.

A squirrel brings snacks while a badger tells jokes,
While the beetles all clink with their tiny puffs of smoke.
The moon sneaks a peek, just to burst into laughs,
At the line dance they do with their twinkling gaffs.

A raccoon performs while the turtles keep beat,
Tunes made of chirps, oh, they can't be discreet!
With each step they twirl, every tail starts to wag,
Creating a spectacle, no room for a brag.

With echoes of giggles and twirls in the air,
They weave through the dusk, light as feathers, they dare.

When dawn starts to rise, they know fun's to be found,
In the heart of the vale, oh so lively and round!

Peregrine's Quest through the Thorns

A peregrine falcon with dreams oh so grand,
Decided to venture to a far-off land.
Through thickets of thorns, he soared high and wide,
With mischief in mind, and a flurry of pride.

He swooped past the brambles with such a sharp grin,
While singing a tune, as if he'd just win.
But thorns called his bluff; he got caught in a mess,
With feathers all tangled, a true fashion stress!

A mouse wandered by with a curious glance,
"Hey there, my friend, want to join in my dance?"
With a flip and a flap, the falcon took flight,
Together they spun, oh what a silly sight!

So a quest turned to fun, beneath thorns they had played,
A tale of misfortunes, yet laughter displayed.
With each little tumble and flurry they spun,
A reminder that joy can be found just for fun!

Tides of the Timeless Wilderness

In the heart of the woods, where the river runs wild,
A otter named Ozzie played tricks like a child.
He'd slip on the banks, causing all kinds of splashes,
Sending everyone swirling, with giggles and dashes.

The cattails all swayed as the fish flopped in fright,
While the frogs jumped in sync, to their own silly fright.
The waves formed a rhythm, the trees hummed along,
In a flood of laughter, they sang nature's song.

With friends gathering round, they laid down for a rest,
As the beaver joined in with construction to test.
But the dam fell apart, what a sight to behold,
With splashes and giggles, the story retold!

Through tides and through time, their mischief they'd share,
In the timeless wilds, with naught but a care.
Joy flows like a river, a boundless delight,
In the laughter of creatures, each day holds a night!

The Mournful Melody of the Marshland

In the marsh, a frog sings loud,
His voice is quite the raucous crowd.
He croaks a tune that's not so sweet,
While nearby, ducks clack their feet.

A raccoon comes with a puzzled look,
Saying, 'That tune's not in my book!'
The dragonflies dance, giggle and spin,
While the turtle just grins with a sly grin.

The reeds sway too, joining the fun,
They sway like dancers under the sun.
A snail slips by with a comical pace,
Trying to keep up in the race.

Then comes the owl, with a wise old laugh,
Saying, 'Now wait, you've lost your path!'
They all laugh and join in the throng,
For in the marsh, no one stays wrong!

Whimsical Whispers of the Wild

A squirrel with nuts of all shapes and sizes,
Found a stash that hid some surprises.
He tripped and fell, what a silly plight,
Rolling down hills, a comical sight.

The butterflies giggle, flutter and sway,
As the hedgehog squeaks, 'Hey, no delay!'
They start a parade, with leaves as their hats,
Even the bumblebees join in with chats.

A rabbit hops in, does a fancy twirl,
Bumping into a chubby old girl.
She squeaks and squeals, they all take flight,
Chasing their tails in pure delight.

In the wild where laughter reigns so bright,
Every step takes a turn, pure delight.
With whispers echoing through the trees,
Joy finds a way, like a playful breeze!

Unveiling the Stories of the Sapphire Streams

Sapphire streams gurgle with secrets untold,
Where fish flash and dance, oh so bold.
A salmon slips, does a wiggly flip,
While otters laugh, taking a dip.

The frogs engage in a ribbiting chat,
Debating on whether they're fish or a cat.
The water lilies nod with a grin,
'You are what you are, where's the sin?'

A bear strolls by, stepping with care,
Knocking down branches, tossing through air.
The giggle of water plays in the sun,
Stories unfold, oh what fun, what fun!

From ripples to bubbles, tales come alive,
Each droplet sharing how creatures thrive.
With a wink and a splash, they call and they scream,
The wild's a new stage, it's all just a dream!

The Dulcet Call of the Dusky Nightingale

The nightingale sings, oh what a delight,
With dulcet tones in the pale moonlight.
But he gets tangled, oh dear what a sight,
In the vines he's become quite the fright.

The cricket joins in, with a chirp and a hop,
Saying, 'Come on, it's time! Don't stop!'
While the fireflies twinkle in light-hearted glee,
Dancing around him, wild and free.

The wise old owl shakes his feathery head,
'Not another tune, enough is said!'
But the nightingale won't let the fun cease,
So they all join in, echoing peace.

With laughter and music reaching the stars,
The creatures all gather, beneath the guitars.
Each note floats high, fills the dusky night,
Celebrating joy until morning's light!

Reflections on a Foggy Dusk

In the damp of the twilight, frogs hold their court,
With croaks like a symphony, a ribbiting sport.
Tadpoles in tuxedos waltz through the green,
While fireflies blink like stars on the scene.

The owls wear their glasses, quite wise and aloof,
Reciting tall tales from the roof of the woof.
Crickets audition for roles in a play,
But all get distracted by cheese on a tray.

A raccoon in a hat juggles worms with a grin,
While the skunks team up, planning their next win.
Laughter erupts from the bushes around,
As the gossiping hedgehogs spin tales profound.

And so in the fog, as the sun bids goodbye,
The creatures erupt with a gleeful cry.
In costumes and colors, they paint the world bright,
A humorous show in the dimming twilight.

The Haunting Melody of Misty Morn

A duck quacks a tune, as it wades through the grass,
While crickets perform in their elegant class.
The mist drapes like lace on the sleepy old bog,
As owls hoot in rhythm, keeping time like a log.

Frogs in the reeds join the morning parade,
With jumps and roundness, they're unafraid.
Squirrels in top hats dance on the lawn,
While a snail in a bowtie takes ages to yawn.

The mist whispers secrets to daisies below,
As the sun giggles softly, starting its show.
A chorus of laughter from creatures nearby,
As a raccoon with flair tries a hand at the sky.

Each note lifts the spirits in playful delight,
While the bog breathes life in the soft morning light.
And though it's quite eerie with shadows galore,
The humor in nature leaves us wanting more.

Tales of the Twisting Thicket

In the thicket, they gather, the bunnies and bears,
Trading tall stories of great, wild affairs.
With whispers of mischief, their fur all a-fluff,
The tales they concoct can be totally stuff.

A fox paints a picture of chasing a hen,
While the owls roll their eyes, thinking 'never again.'
The pine trees lean in, curious to hear,
Of squabbles and fumbles that turn into cheer.

A hedgehog narrates how he won a grand race,
While a turtle disputes from the back of the place.
They laugh and they shout, each one with their grip,
Admiring the skills of their friend who can flip.

And just as the sun sets, they drink from a cup,
Filled with dew drops and berries, they fill it right up.
In the twisting thicket, where stories outshine,
Laughter rings out, and the world feels divine.

Dances by the Moonlit Pond

When the moon lifts her skirt, all the frogs know to sway,
In a dance by the pond, they jive and they play.
With splashes and leaps, they don't seem to care,
The fish roll their eyes at the chaos they share.

A raccoon leads movement with a whimsical spin,
While dragonflies buzz, both dizzy and thin.
The turtles don sunglasses, all hip and so cool,
Watching the antics, they play it by rule.

As the crickets provide the percussion and beat,
The pond shimmers brightly where waters do meet.
A lone catfish glares, a bit grumpy and pensive,
While the entire shindig feels utterly senseless.

Laughter erupts with each croak and each splash,
As friends under starlight enjoy the grand bash.
So twirl with the frogs, let your worries take flight,
In the moonlit reflections, everything feels right.

The Sorrowful Serenade of the Swamp

In a bog where the frogs croak loud,
A turtle lost his way and bowed.
With a hat made of lily, quite the sight,
He mourned for snacks he'd miss tonight.

The gnarled trees giggle, what a show,
As a crab in a bowtie steals the glow.
A heron lands, struts with flair,
Then slips on mud, flies through the air!

The alligators sigh, we can't compete,
With a singing frog who can't find his beat.
They gather 'round for the greatest of fun,
But the bug choir is muted—oh what a run!

Oh, the swamp holds secrets, jokes it decides,
Like the time a raccoon wore moonlight strides.
In the echo of cackles, we find our release,
Laughter quakes the marsh—oh sweet swampy peace.

Fables from the Forgotten Fen

In a fen where the whispers intertwine,
Lived a mouse who thought he could dine on wine.
His cheese dreams floated, like clouds on a breeze,
But ended with mustard and ants in the cheese!

A badger recited his scholarly tales,
While a frog added flair with his fancy pails.
Yet the night grew plump with mischievous glee,
As fireflies danced to the badger's decree.

Amidst the reeds, a raccoon wore socks,
Singing of fish caught in rickety docks.
With laughter erupting, they'd all share a bite,
And mock the moon's beam for playing too bright.

So gather, dear friends, in the fen's lively light,
Where the stories swirl like a comical kite.
The fables are funny, with a twist here and there,
In the heart of this nook, we find joy everywhere!

The Echoing Heartbeat of the Night

When the stars blink and the moon turns round,
The crickets begin their nocturnal sound.
A raccoon steals snacks from the picnic spread,
While owls roll their eyes, wishing they'd fled.

The fireflies twinkle, a bright little show,
As a turtle, confused, thinks they're friends, oh no!
He wobbles and tumbles right into a heap,
Startling the bullfrogs, who giggle, then leap.

The marsh is alive with the silliest sights,
As the hedgehog on stilts takes a turn in the lights.
He stumbles and fumbles, creating a fright,
A ruckus erupts in the gobbling night.

With laughter like echoes that bounce off the trees,
The night plays a game, floating soft on the breeze.
In this whimsical world, where joy is our right,
We dance with the darkness, our hearts burning bright.

Dreams Drifting over the Dappled Dell

In a dell where the daisies all giggle and sway,
A rabbit hops by in a curious way.
He juggles some carrots, what a brave feat!
But loses a lettuce, oh what a sweet treat!

A fox claims it's minted, a salad so new,
But a slug in a tux said, "That won't do!"
They squabble and scramble, quite the ruckus, indeed,
As squirrels toss acorns, planting a seed.

With shadows that dance, and laughter that's bright,
A hedgehog recites poems to the cool night.
His audience, giggling, can't take it just yet,
As the jokes start to tumble—a humorous fret!

Beneath the old trees, where the breezes hum low,
The dreams swirl in laughter, oh what a glow!
In the heart of the dell, joy sings like a bell,
With oddball adventures—we bid you farewell!

Murmurs from the Misty Hollow

In a hollow where the critters play,
Frogs sing loudly, hippos sway.
A turtle wears a jaunty hat,
And dreams of being a dancing cat.

The fireflies all glow in style,
As raccoons laugh and dance a while.
The owl hoots jokes with wise delight,
While shadows jive beneath the light.

A snail ran past, oh what a race!
It lost and moped with such a face.
The bushes chuckle, swaying low,
As laughter spreads, a vibrant show.

So come and join this merry throng,
In the hollow where we all belong.
Leave your worries far behind,
And find the joy in what you find.

The Ballad Within the Brambles.

In brambles thick, a squirrel sings,
About his lost and found new things.
He saw a nut, it rolled away,
And led him on a wild ballet.

A hedgehog pranced with tiny shoes,
Spinning tales of other critters' blues.
With every turn, he'd wobble and sway,
Making the bushes giggle and play.

A porcupine joined in, quite bold,
With a dance move that never gets old.
He swept the floor with prickly flair,
The brambles echoing his fancy air.

So if you pass these thorny lanes,
Just listen for the laughter strains.
For in the thicket, wonders dwell,
And silly stories they will tell.

Whispers of the Wildwood

In wildwood woods, the creatures chat,
About a dog who chased his hat.
The hat flew high, a kite of sorts,
While the cat laughed from her tree fort.

A mischievous raccoon planned a prank,
To put a frog inside a tank.
But frogs don't swim, they jump and croak,
The raccoon laughed, this wasn't a joke!

The deer held court, a comical sight,
As they debated who jumped the height.
Their tails a-swishing, they exchanged jives,
In this wood where humor thrives.

So stroll beneath the towering trees,
And join the fun, a laugh with ease.
For in the wildwood, jesters play,
And keep your worries far at bay.

Echoes from the Eldergrove

In the eldritch grove where echoes ring,
A fox named Fred started to sing.
He serenaded the moonlit night,
With howls that gave the stars a fright.

The rabbits joined, in hops they spun,
A jig so lively, oh what fun!
With fluffy tails and twitchy noses,
They danced amid the blooming roses.

A wise old turtle joined the crew,
With tales of days when skies were blue.
But every story took a twist,
That left the owls and bats quite pissed.

Echoes laugh in the silvery mist,
As creatures share their joking list.
In the grove, where joy won't cease,
Come find a moment, and dance in peace.

Moonbeams on the Glistening Quagmire

In the dark, frogs croon a tune,
With moonbeams dancing 'round like a loon.
The fireflies wink, they tease, they zoom,
While critters gather for a marshy boom.

A turtle in shades sips tea with flair,
Bragging of races without a care.
While snails on stilts pratfall, oh so grand,
Painted by the glow, like a master plan.

The raccoons in tuxes hold a grand ball,
As the mud pies are served by a squirrel so tall.
Hilarity reigns, so wild and free,
In this quagmire world, laughter's the key.

But watch your step, you might take a dive,
With muddy high jinks, we're all alive!
The bog's quite the place for whimsical dreams,
As giggles fill the air, bursting at the seams.

The Tanglewood Chronicles

In Tanglewood trees, where the shadows lurk,
A hedgehog plays chess, he's such a quirk.
With a toad as his rival, both puffed with pride,
The pieces are mushrooms, each one a guide.

The owls in the branches hoot jokes on repeat,
While the rabbits do cartwheels, oh so fleet.
A wise old owl trips over a sprig,
And everyone cackles, it's quite the gig.

With mushrooms for chairs, the critters all gather,
Telling tall tales that make the trees chatter.
A fox brings snacks, but they're all just air,
He swears they're gourmet, but we just stare.

As night blankets all in the softest grey,
The laughter and jest keep the goblins at bay.
In this tangled realm where tomfoolery thrives,
You'll find the best stories and chuckles that jive.

The Serpent's Waterway Ballad

In the snake's winding path, there's a giddy spree,
With fishy performers in a splashy lea.
A catfish in boots sings high on a log,
While the crabs do a jig on a soggy bog.

The serpent with swagger glides through the muck,
Playing tricks on the frogs, who are all out of luck.
He twirls and he twines, making quite the show,
While the otters just chuckle, 'Hey, watch him go!'

A riddle contest forms under the stars,
With wise old turtles sporting herculean scars.
Alongside the reeds, they exchange silly jests,
As the waterway sings with its funny quests.

But is that a splash? Oh dear, what a sight!
A frog in a tutu takes flight in the night.
In the spiral of laughter, everyone sings,
In the serpent's grand dance, joy always springs.

Songs of the Marshland Spirits

In the marshland low, where the spirits play,
They giggle and shrug the dullness away.
With bog sprites in bloom, all twinkling with glee,
They dance on the lily pads, wild and free.

A wisp in a hat leads a merry parade,
With shadows that shimmy, not one is dismayed.
A group of young minnows spins round and round,
Creating a whirlpool of laughter profound.

With whispers of magic that twine through the air,
The critters join in with a curious flair.
The frogs play the drums, while the raccoons sing,
A symphony carried by the blooms of spring.

As the moon rises high, they toast with old reeds,
Exchanging sweet stories of hopes and good deeds.
In the glow of the night, with spirits alight,
The marshland sings songs that feel just right.

Tales by the Twilight Stream

At twilight's edge, the frogs convene,
They croak their tales, a silly scene.
With every leap, they swap a jest,
A championship of ribbits, at their best.

The fireflies dance, with giggles bright,
Showing off their moves, a fleeting sight.
They flicker like stars, tiny and fast,
In this bubbly bog, hilarity lasts.

A turtle joins, with a swagger fine,
Claiming he's slow, but oh, he's divine!
He tells of adventures, how he won a race,
But with his shell, he can't keep pace.

So gather 'round, let laughter flow,
In twilight's embrace, let fun bestow.
For when nature giggles, so should we,
At this comical stream, carefree and free.

Shadows on the Mossy Path

On the mossy path, shadows play,
A raccoon wearing glasses, what can I say?
He reads a map, lost in the mist,
Claiming he's found the perfect tryst.

A hedgehog squeaks, with a pinprick taunt,
Saying, "I'm sharp! You can't daunt!"
But when he trips, oh what a sight,
Rolling in laughter, he took flight!

The owl above hoots out a cheer,
Bobbing his head, he's quite sincere.
His headphones on, tunes blaring loud,
In this forest, he's truly proud.

As shadows stretch, they waltz and slip,
Each twist and turn, a comical trip.
In laughter's embrace, these creatures abide,
On the mossy path, where fun can't hide.

The Owl's Midnight Serenade

The owls in the trees, oh what a crew,
Singing off-key, but they think it's cool.
With every hoot, a giggle we find,
Their midnight serenade, truly unrefined.

They flap their wings, in an awkward dance,
One fell out of rhythm, missed his chance.
With feathers ruffled and faces askew,
They find their groove in the deep midnight dew.

An old toad croaks, trying to join,
With a voice so deep, it's quite the conjoined!
"To my beat," he sings, "you must adhere!"
But ends up croaking, "Hoo, I'm here!"

Under the moon, the laughter grows,
All creatures chuckle, as the hooting flows.
In this whimsical night, joy takes flight,
With the owls serenading, till morning light.

Dreams of the Humming Marsh

In the humming marsh, where the critters dream,
A snail with ideas, or so it would seem.
He pitches inventions, with a slow-motion flair,
Like a pogo stick, but with more air!

The dragonflies buzz, with a cheeky grin,
Challenging frogs, saying, "Let's begin!"
With leapfrog bets on who can jump high,
They laugh as they splash, oh my, oh my!

A whimsical dance-off, starts in the reeds,
Each one showing off their wildest deeds.
A turtle twerks with his shell so round,
While the otters roll with laughter abound.

So join this marsh, where dreams take flight,
Amid giggles and grins, the mood feels just right.
In nature's comedy, we find our cheer,
In the dreams of the marsh, we hold dear.

The Gnarled Roots of Remembering

In a bog where stories bloom,
The gnarled roots play tricks and loom.
A frog in a suit struts with flair,
While turtles gossip in the air.

With fireflies dancing a jig so bright,
They'll tell you tales deep into the night.
Of socks on trees and hats on ducks,
In this quirky land of silly luck.

Memories twist like the old oak's knot,
Each branches' tale funny, not forgot.
A raccoon's laugh echoes with glee,
As he steals snacks from the wild blueberry.

So join in the laughter, take a seat,
In the bog where the playful creatures meet.
Where roots and dreams mischievously play,
And everyone smiles as they frolic away.

Fables Wrapped in Ferns

Among the ferns, stories weave,
Of clumsy owls that just won't leave.
An army of ants with boots so neat,
Marching to rhythms of wiggly feet.

Fairies giggle, their wings aglow,
As they prank the snail moving slow.
A wise old toad with a crooked grin,
Sings ballads of mischief, let the fun begin!

Chasing shadows, a fox in disguise,
Wearing a hat that's too large for his eyes.
In a world where laughter reigns supreme,
Every fable, a whimsical dream.

So wander these woods of oddities grand,
Where giggles and tales go hand in hand.
Each fable wrapped in nature's embrace,
Is a chance for joy in this curious place.

Skyward Haze and Grounded Dreams

Beneath the haze, laughter resounds,
As clouds play hopscotch on skies unbound.
A squirrel in stripes sketches the air,
While dreaming of adventures, light as a feather.

Bunnies bounce on mushrooms so spry,
Reciting poems to birds that fly.
A hedgehog plays sax with sweet notes,
Filling the bog with melodious quotes.

While stars poke fun at the moon's shy glow,
They giggle at dreams that ebb and flow.
The grounded creatures spread their cheer,
In a world where laughter pulls you near.

So let's raise our cups to the skyward haze,
And dance beneath the laughter's gaze.
For in this quirk of nature's gleam,
Life is a delightful and silly dream.

The Ethereal Mist's Chronicle

In the mist that twirls like soft cotton,
A humor-filled world is begotten.
With each foggy swirl, silly shapes appear,
A laughing cat playing hide and cheer.

Ghostly echoes with giggles abound,
Frisky spirits leap from the ground.
They tell tales of feasts with bubblegum pies,
And roast marshmallows under starlit skies.

A dance of the fog with a mischievous wink,
As a squirrel sips nectar from the brink.
The night wraps stories with laughter so grand,
In the misty veil where jokes expand.

So step into shadows where giggles reside,
And let the silly secrets be your guide.
In the ethereal mist, old tales delight,
Unraveling joy in the heart of the night.

The Enigma of the Eldritch Meadow

In the meadow's twisty paths,
A dancing duck quite full of sass,
He quacked a tune both soft and loud,
While muddy frogs formed quite the crowd.

With every hop, a secret hides,
The daisies giggle, nature's guides,
A snail in shades thinks he's a star,
While butterflies gather, near and far.

A sprite with shoes that squeak and squeal,
Tricks the ox to spin and reel,
While honeybees claim royal thrones,
In secret meetings near old stones.

But as the sun begins to fade,
The creatures join this charming parade,
With laughter echoing all around,
The meadow's magic knows no bound.

Whims of the Wandering Willow

By the willow, tales unfold,
Where giggling squirrels brave and bold,
Claim acorns spicy, all for fun,
And chase their shadows 'til they run.

The branches whisper silly rhymes,
As sunbeams tickle feet in climes,
A rabbit juggles three ripe pears,
While froggies cheer from their wet lairs.

The gossiping leaves share their taste,
Of pies made from the world's finest paste,
While owls debate who's lost the plot,
Chewing on thoughts that hit the spot.

When twilight paints the sky in glee,
The willow sways, it's wild and free,
With laughter drawing in the stars,
Adventures wait, no need for cars.

The Cry of the Courageous Crickets

Though small in size, they sing with might,
   Under moon's glow, a charming sight,
   With tiny swords made out of grass,
   They duel and laugh, oh what a class!

   A cricket clad in shades of green,
   Claims he's the bravest ever seen,
   While others roll in fits of glee,
   At tales of his grand victory.

   Each chirp a call, a daring feat,
   As fireflies dance on tiny feet,
   The nighttime buzz, a lively chat,
   As legends grow of what they're at.

But as dawn breaks, they take a pause,
   For sleepy thoughts and tiny jaws,
They nestle down 'neath leaves once more,
   Dreaming of fights, and leaps, and lore.

Lost in the Lullaby of Lucent Leaves

In the forest's hug, a whisper hums,
Where bouncing bunnies laugh like drums,
They spin 'round trees and leap on logs,
While snickering owls play tricks on frogs.

The leaves above, a shimm'ring choir,
As silly songs bring joy, inspire,
The scrappy winds blow tunes askew,
While chipmunks join, with nutty stew.

A turtle wearing a sunhat bright,
Claims he's the prince of this delight,
And as the sun begins to gleam,
The forest stirs, awash with dream.

But come the dusk, the laughter fades,
As nature's party slowly wades,
Yet in their hearts, the fun secured,
For laughter lives, forever blurred.

Chronicles of the Breezy Meadow

In a field where the daisies dance,
A goat tried to wear a bright yellow pants.
He tripped on a blade, oh what a sight,
Rolling down hills, in pure delight.

The flowers all giggled, the sun was so bright,
As the goat flipped and flopped, full of spite.
"Who wears pants?" the bees all buzzed,
While the butterflies laughed, all in a fuzz.

A squirrel joined in, with acorn in hand,
Said, "Goat, let's start a fashion brand!"
They pranced and they danced, in quite the parade,
Making wild outfits from leaves, unafraid.

So if you wander through meadows so wide,
Look for the goat with his quirky pride.
He may sway in the wind, with no care at all,
For laughter is wealth—come one, come all!

Shadows Cast by the Luminous Glow

Under the stars, the frogs start to croak,
While shadows of crickets, they dance and they poke.
A lantern hung low, casting light on the ground,
And a raccoon pranced in, making quite the sound.

He wore a top hat, with swagger so bold,
Claiming the night with stories retold.
"I once met a wizard who lost his way,
He turned my tail blue—what a wild display!"

The fireflies flickered, they joined in the fun,
While the owl hooted loud, calling everyone.
What trick will they play in the deep of the night?
A conga line forms—a waltz full of fright!

So next time you gaze at the glow of the moon,
Join in the laughter, don't wait until noon.
The shadows may dance, but they also can sing,
In the silliness found when the night's at its swing!

The Untold Stories of the Wandering Breeze

A gust through the trees told secrets so sweet,
Of the mailman squirrel who feared his own feet.
He tripped on a branch, with a package in hand,
Sending letters a-flying all over the land.

Each note was a riddle, a giggle of glee,
"Why did the chicken, cross over to me?"
The breeze couldn't stop rolling in laughter so free,
As the squirrel looked puzzled, his cheeks turning brie.

But a robin took charge, with a tweet and a hop,
"To help with the mail, let's have a big pop!"
So they laughed through the trees, made a grand festive day,
While the letters all tumbled, in a whimsical way.

So when in the woods, if you hear the wind play,
Remember the squirrel who lost his bouquet.
For laughter and joy are just whisked on a breeze,
And stories unfold, like the rustling leaves!

Secrets of the Serene Stream

In the glimmering waters, fish gather to chat,
About a big cat that wore a bright hat.
The stories they told, made them giggle and splash,
As frogs leapt around, bringing joy in a flash.

"Did you see him slip?" a goldfish exclaimed,
"He skidded on mud; oh, what a shame!"
A ripple of laughter, it spread like a song,
While the stream danced along, where all tales belong.

A turtle so wise, he nodded along,
Said, "This silly cat, he surely is wrong.
To flaunt such a hat in the mud and the muck,
Is to tempt all the puddles—oh, wish him good luck!"

So if by the stream, you hear giggles and glee,
Join in the fun, oh come, take a seat!
For nature has secrets, and laughter can teem,
In the bubbling waters, and the joy of a dream!

Whispers of the Wistful Wren

In the thicket, a wren sings sweet,
Chirping tales of a tiny beet,
With a wink and a hop, he'll strut so fine,
Telling secrets of the great pine.

A frog in the pond gives a loud croak,
As the wren giggles and teases the bloke,
"Hey there, my friend, don't jump too high,
You might land on a lily and fly!"

The dragonflies dance, with a flutter and flare,
Chasing the wren in the warm summer air,
"Catch me if you can!" the tiny bird beams,
While the frog rolls his eyes, lost in his dreams.

By twilight, the wren calls out his tune,
Tickling the stars, a bright, shiny balloon,
With laughter so light, it carries on air,
Making all creatures stop, and just stare.

The Echoing Journey

Through the meadows, a chorus rings,
A troupe of critters with fanciful things,
A tortoise in slippers and a squirrel on a bike,
Decide to unite for a wild little hike.

They trip and they tumble, oh what a scene,
With splashes of color in vibrant sheen,
A snail with a helmet takes the front lead,
While the rabbit just hops, playing catch-up with speed.

"Why hurry?" quips tortoise, slow as can be,
"The grass is just right for us all to see!"
With giggles and snickers, they stop for a snack,
Gorging on mushrooms – they all double back!

At dusk, they sit sharing whimsical tales,
Of giants in puddles and fish with long scales,
Their laughter resonates, a melodious song,
Echoing hilarity all night long.

Starlight on the Muddy Waters

Under the moon, the critters convene,
With a party to claim in the soft, silver sheen,
A raccoon in glasses, a cat with a hat,
Start sharing their dreams while a frog plays the spat.

Splashing in puddles, they dance on the ground,
With laughter so loud, it echoes around,
A firefly flickers, a starry young gnome,
Shouting, "Let's celebrate! This mud is our home!"

The otter brings snacks in a tiny canoe,
As chickens in boots start a conga, it's true,
With a squeal and a tilt, they glide with delight,
In moonlit shenanigans that last till the night.

With joy in their hearts, they sway and they spin,
For in muddy waters, there's fun to be in,
So join in the frolic, leave worries behind,
In starlight and laughter, pure joy you will find.

The Raven's Melancholy

A raven of gloom sits high on a branch,
Watching the critters; they play, what a chance,
With feathers all ruffled and eyes full of plight,
He squawks at the bunnies, "Where's all the light?"

A skunk passes by with a flower on top,
Singing about woes and a tantalizing flop,
"Cheer up, dear friend, life's not all gray,
Join us for fun, chase that frown away!"

The raven just sighs, "But I'm supposed to brood,
What if I cry and spoil all your food?"
A porcupine chuckles, "Well, that's quite a tale,
Slap on a smile, and you'd still prevail!"

So he fluffs out his feathers and gives it a go,
With a cackle and caw, he steals the whole show,
In the midst of their joy, he forgets his dread,
And dances with laughter, the gloom he must shed.

Whispers Through the Willow Woods

In the woods where the willows sway,
A rabbit danced, hip-hip-hooray!
He tripped on a root, went tumbling down,
And wore a parade of leaves like a crown.

Squirrels giggled from high up in the trees,
As he shook off the twigs with the greatest of ease.
"Next time I'll prance with a little more grace!"
But a grin on his face couldn't be erased.

The wise old owl, with a wink and a clap,
Said, "Bunny dear, you could use a nap!"
But the rabbit just laughed, with a glint in his eye,
"I'll nap when I'm done being the star in the sky!"

So round went the rabbit, a dance full of cheer,
With a band of frogs croaking loud in his ear.
The night drew on, and the stars shined bright,
While the woods echoed laughter 'til morning light.

Secrets Beneath the Starlit Fen

In the fen where the fireflies glow,
A dancing frog stole the show!
He slipped on a leaf, gave a comic shout,
And landed with splat, oh what a clout!

The dragonflies buzzed, a dazzling crowd,
"What a performer!" they cheered out loud.
"Encore! Encore!" came the cries from the reeds,
As the froggy star bowed, fulfilling their needs.

But oh, in the shadows creep tipsy old newts,
With stories of swamp and ancient loot.
"We found a treasure, worth far more than gold!"
They chuckled and whispered, their tales of old.

Yet each time they spoke, they forgot what they said,
Claiming they'd lost it, oh, folly instead!
With giggles and wiggles, the fen turned to glee,
As secrets of laughter came floating to me.

Echoes in the Enchanted Marsh

In the marsh where the will-o'-the-wisps weave,
    A plump little otter decided to grieve.
    He lost his favorite shiny, round ball,
And he wailed like a babe, to the croaking thrall.

The cattails all rustled, and frogs huddled near,
"Don't cry little otter, let's give you a cheer!"
So they started a tune, with a splash and a croak,
    Until even the moon felt joy in the joke.

Then out from a bulrush, a wise turtle peeked,
"Your ball is right here, you silly, you squeaked!"
    With a flick of a fin and a little round grin,
    The otter jumped up, squealed with a spin.

All creatures rejoiced as they danced in the light,
    An otter with treasure, no longer in fright.
They basked in the glow, filling marsh with delight,
    In echoes of laughter, a joyous goodnight.

The Lament of the Lost Firefly

In the twilight's embrace, a firefly wept,
He lost his bright glow, oh how he felt inept!
He shone like a lantern, but now was so dim,
"How will I light up the night?" he whimpered on whim.

The crickets all laughed with a chirpy delight,
"Just dance like a madman, you'll sparkle tonight!"
"But I can hardly twinkle, I'm heavy with gloom!"
The firefly sighed, sinking low in the bloom.

Then a wise little spider spun webs with great care,
"A flicker of joy can light up the air!"
With a twirl and a spin, the firefly took flight,
Humming and buzzing, he found his lost light.

From garden to garden, all creatures adored,
As he zipped and he zoomed, his brightness restored.
The firefly giggled with friends in the glade,
For sometimes it takes a dance to unshade.

Legends of the Moonlit Marsh

In the marsh where the frogs croak loud,
A ghost in a tutu danced on a cloud.
He tripped on some moss, fell flat on his face,
While crickets all chuckled, 'What a fine grace!'

The owls spun tales of a fish in a hat,
Who claimed he could sing like a chubby old cat.
But splashing about, he could only make noise,
Leaving the marsh with a bunch of wet boys!

A snail with a shell made of foil so bright,
Announced to the fireflies, 'I'm fast as a kite!'
But slow as a drip, he surprised all around,
As he inch-wormed away, he whispered, 'I'm bound!'

So gather your friends for a night full of mirth,
In the moonlit marsh of peculiar birth.
Where laughter and giggles rise up to the sky,
And the legends are silly, oh me, oh my!

The Bramble's Lament

In brambles and thickets, a wise old toad,
Complained of the thorns as a heavy load.
He croaked to the breeze, 'It's a prickly affair!'
While all of the hedgehogs just giggled with flair.

'Oh, dance with me, friends,' called a cheeky old quail,
'We'll boogie through bramble and sing without fail!'
But tripping on twigs, they collapsed in a heap,
With snickers and snorts, their joy deep and steep.

A rabbit named Benny wore shoes made of hay,
Claimed he could hop on a bright sunny day.
Yet caught by a bramble, he twirled in surprise,
Leaving all his friends with wide-open eyes.

The bramble just chuckled, 'Oh look at this crew,
All tangled and laughing; that's what I do!'
So dance through the thicket, let laughter resound,
For life's greatest joys are in friendship found.

Secrets Beneath the Swamp Sky

Beneath the swamp sky where the willows sway,
A gator named Gary had much to say.
With a hat made of lily and a cane of a reed,
He declared, 'I'm the king, so attend to my creed!'

But the critters just snickered, 'Oh Gary, you fool,
For beneath that grand title, you still swim in drool!'
And with snorts and some snickers, they rolled on the ground,
While Gary just grumbled, 'Oh, why can't I be sound?'

The catfish all giggled and splashed through the muck,
Singing songs of the gator, 'He thinks he's in luck!'
Yet with each silly blunder, they wiggled with glee,
For secrets can bubble where laughter runs free.

So join in the fun under stars that all twinkle,
Where secrets unfold and the frogs never wrinkle.
In the swampy embrace, let your heart find its beat,
With smiles and surprises, it's laughter we greet!

The Enchanted Thicket's Song

In an enchanted thicket where the shadows glow,
A squirrel named Nibbles put on quite a show.
With acorn confetti and a cap full of tricks,
He juggled ripe berries that left all in kicks.

The owls in their wisdom proclaimed him a star,
While the raccoons danced round with a float made of tar.

Yet every sweet move led to topsy-turvy fun,
As Nibbles slipped once and sent berries to run!

The hedgehogs all chuckled, 'Now that's quite a sight,
A squirrel with a flair for a laughable plight!'
And Nibbles just winked, 'It's the fun that I bring,
You laugh your best laughs when your heart starts to sing!'

So wander the thicket, let your joy freely play,
In the magic of laughter, we'll dance the night away.
For in forests enchanted, love and joy both belong,
And shadows all twinkle to the thicket's sweet song!

www.ingramcontent.com/pod-product-compliance
Lightning Source LLC
Chambersburg PA
CBHW072142200426
43209CB00051B/272